core belief™

Bible Study Series
for junior high/middle school

THE TRUTH ABOUT The Last Days

Group
Loveland, Colorado

The Truth About The Last Days

Core Belief Bible Study Series

Credits

Editor: Karl Leuthauser
Creative Development Editor: Paul Woods
Chief Creative Officer: Joani Schultz
Copy Editor: Pamela Shoup
Art Director: Ray Tollison
Cover Art Director: Jeff A. Storm
Photographer: Craig DeMartino
Production Manager: Gingar Kunkel

ISBN 0-7644-0864-X
10 9 8 7 6 5 4 3 2 1   07 06 05 04 03 02 01 00 99 98

Printed in the United States of America.

core belief

Bible Study Series
for junior high/middle school

contents:

the Core Belief: The Last Days

Some say we're in the Last Days right now. Some say we've been in the Last Days for two thousand years. Regardless of your opinion about the Last Days, you need to help your students prepare for them. If they don't, they won't be going to heaven with Jesus. Instead, they'll spend an eternity separated from God.

Someday Christ will return to earth in power and glory. We don't know the day or the hour, but we'd better be ready. He'll make it clear who deserves punishment and who deserves reward. Then he'll gather all his people, those who are alive and those who have died, and take them to be with him. And God will create a new heaven and a new earth for us to live in forever.

the Helpful Stuff

the ▼Studies

▼The Last Days as a Core Christian Belief

When kids have a big test coming at school, they want to know all about it: What's going to be covered, when it will be, and how thoroughly they're expected to know the material. They want to be ready.

In the same way, kids need to know the pertinent details of the Last Days to help them be ready for Jesus' return. No one knows the exact date or time Jesus will return, but the Bible does give us solid information about what is to happen.

The Last Days are all about hope for creation and for all those who trust in Christ. Christians look forward to rewards and to an existence in the presence of God. The church looks forward to the defeat of Satan and to the coming kingdom. And all creation looks forward to cleansing and redemption—a new heaven and earth.

In the first study of *The Truth About the Last Days,* kids will look at the benefits that will follow Jesus' return. They'll discuss **natural disasters** and the helplessness and confusion that accompany such events. The investigation will help kids realize that every type of disaster will end when Christ returns, because God is creating a new heaven and earth for Christians.

The second study will help clear up some of the confusion your kids may have about the Last Days. The study will help students discover what biblical **prophecy** clearly shows is in store for Christians by highlighting the truth that Christ will return someday to judge the world.

The third study will remind kids to prepare for eternity. Your students may witness Christ's second coming while they're still alive, or they may meet him face to face when they die. You'll teach kids that Jesus has provided an opportunity for eternal life and that they can be ready to meet Jesus—whether they meet him through his return or through **death.**

The final study will encourage kids to make the most of the time and the **talents** God has given them. You'll challenge them to live with purpose and deliberate action because Christ could return at any time.

Knowing that Jesus is returning for us someday gives us hope when things look hopeless in our lives. And it motivates us to be faithful to him, so that when he returns he won't be disappointed in us. Your kids need the hope that Jesus gives and the encouragement to be faithful as they look for the signs of the Last Days occurring all around them.

For a more comprehensive look at this Core Christian Belief, read Group's **Get Real: Making Core Christian Beliefs Relevant to Teenagers.**

DEPTHFINDER

To help you effectively guide your kids toward this Core Christian Belief, use these overviews as a launching point for a more in-depth study of the last days.

There is a lot we don't know for sure about Jesus' second coming, but we do know that he *is* coming! Christians disagree on many details of the Second Coming, but there are also many things on which most agree:

- **Most people will physically die before Christ returns.** Everyone except those who are alive at the time of Christ's return will die a physical death. However, in death the human soul doesn't die or "sleep." Everyone who dies will remain conscious, though separate from the body, from the time of his or her death until the final resurrection. Those who are in Christ exist in a state of joy; those not in Christ exist in a state of suffering (Luke 16:19-31; 2 Corinthians 5:1-10; Philippians 1:23; Revelation 14:13).

- **Only God knows exactly when Jesus will return.** Scripture makes it clear that no human can know the exact time of Jesus' return. Thus, we're to live each day as if it might be the day that he is coming for us. Though different views of the Last Days give different outlooks on when Jesus will come, most interpretations leave room for Jesus to return at any time to take Christians to live with him (Mark 13:32; 2 Thessalonians 2:1-3; Titus 2:13; James 5:8-9; 1 Peter 4:7; 2 Peter 3:3-12; 1 John 2:28; Revelation 22:12, 20).

- **Certain events will precede Christ's return.** The Bible predicts the spread of the gospel and the growth of the church before Jesus is to return. However, in the Last Days many people will be consumed with their own pleasures, rejecting or ignoring God. Most believe that some type of antichrist will come and lead a vast following away from Christianity (Matthew 13:31-32; 24:5, 11-12, 14, 24; Colossians 1:23b; 2 Thessalonians 2:3-4, 7-8; 2 Timothy 3:1-5; 2 Peter 3:3-12; 1 John 2:18, 22).

- **Jesus will come in power and glory.** In the Old Testament, predictions of Jesus' coming basically fall into two categories: prophecies concerning a suffering servant and prophecies concerning a victorious king. The first time Jesus came, it was as the suffering servant; the second time it will be as the conquering king. Jesus has already defeated Satan through his death and resurrection, but Satan is still being allowed to rule on earth. At just the right time, Jesus will return to take over his kingdom and destroy all that Satan represents (Isaiah 9:6-7; 53:1-12; Matthew 12:28-29; 24:29-30; 2 Corinthians 4:4; 2 Peter 3:7, 10; Revelation 19:16; 20:11-15).

● **Jesus will come to take Christians to be with him forever.** Throughout the New Testament, writers look with great anticipation toward Jesus' second coming. In the midst of persecution, the writers of the New Testament looked forward to Jesus' return to free them from their suffering. We're told that he'll come suddenly, surprising many, to take Christians to heaven with him. The faithful of the Old Testament and Christians who have died will rise first to meet him, and then those who are still alive will rise to meet him in the sky. The Bible tells us that our time with Jesus will never end. Christians will spend all of eternity in joyous celebration with him (Matthew 24:36-42; John 14:3; Acts 1:10-11; 1 Thessalonians 4:15-17; 5:1-6; Titus 2:13).

● **Jesus will come in judgment.** At Jesus' second coming, many people will be sent to eternal punishment. The judgments that occur when Jesus returns will include the sentencing of those who have rejected faith in God through Jesus as well as the judgment of those who believe. However, the judgment of those who believe will not be to determine any punishment, but to determine rewards (Matthew 25:31-46; 1 Corinthians 3:11-15; 2 Corinthians 5:10; Revelation 20:11-15).

● **Jesus will come to complete the establishment of his kingdom.** While he was on earth, Jesus spoke frequently of the Kingdom of heaven being near. Some feel that the Kingdom was initiated through the church at Jesus' first coming, and will be fulfilled at the second coming. Whatever a person's view of the millennium, people agree that after Jesus' return he will rule over the new heaven and the new earth as King, with Christians ruling with him (Matthew 3:2; Luke 22:28-30; John 18:36; Revelation 21:1-2; 22:5).

Knowing that Jesus is returning for us someday gives us hope when things look hopeless in our lives. And it motivates us to be faithful to him, so that when he returns he won't be disappointed in us. Your kids need the hope that Jesus gives and the encouragement to be faithful as they look for the signs of the Last Days occurring all around them.

CORE CHRISTIAN BELIEF OVERVIEW

Here are the twenty-four Core Christian Belief categories that form the backbone of Core Belief Bible Study Series:

The Nature of God	Jesus Christ	The Holy Spirit
Humanity	Evil	Suffering
Creation	The Spiritual Realm	The Bible
Salvation	Spiritual Growth	Personal Character
God's Justice	Sin & Forgiveness	The Last Days
Love	The Church	Worship
Authority	Prayer	Family
Service	Relationships	Sharing Faith

Look for Group's Core Belief Bible Study Series books in these other Core Christian Beliefs!

about

Bible Study Series
for junior high/middle school

Think for a moment about your young people. When your students walk out of your youth program after they graduate from junior high or high school, what do you want them to know? What foundation do you want them to have so they can make wise choices?

You probably want them to know the essentials of the Christian faith. You want them to base everything they do on the foundational truths of Christianity. Are you meeting this goal?

If you have any doubt that your kids will walk into adulthood knowing and living by the tenets of the Christian faith, then you've picked up the right book. All the books in Group's Core Belief Bible Study Series encourage young people to discover the essentials of Christianity and to put those essentials into practice. Let us explain...

What Is Group's Core Belief Bible Study Series?

Group's Core Belief Bible Study Series is a biblically in-depth study series for junior high and senior high teenagers. This Bible study series utilizes four defining commitments to create each study. These "plumb lines" provide structure and continuity for every activity, study, project, and discussion. They are:

● **A Commitment to Biblical Depth**—Core Belief Bible Study Series is founded on the belief that kids not only *can* understand the deeper truths of the Bible but also *want* to understand them. Therefore, the activities and studies in this series strive to explain the "why" behind every truth we explore. That way, kids learn principles, not just rules.

● **A Commitment to Relevance**—Most kids aren't interested in abstract theories or doctrines about the universe. They want to know how to live successfully right now, today, in the heat of problems they can't ignore. Because of this, each study connects a real-life need with biblical principles that speak directly to that need. This study series finally bridges the gap between Bible truths and the real-world issues kids face.

● **A Commitment to Variety**—Today's young people have been raised in a sound bite world. They demand variety. For that reason, no two meetings in this study series are shaped exactly the same.

● **A Commitment to Active and Interactive Learning**—Active learning is learning by doing. Interactive learning simply takes active learning a step further by having kids teach each other what they've learned. It's a process that helps kids internalize and remember their discoveries.

For a more detailed description of these concepts, see the section titled "Why Active and Interactive Learning Works With Teenagers" beginning on page 57.

So how can you accomplish all this in a set of four easy-to-lead Bible studies? By weaving together various "power" elements to produce a fun experience that leaves kids challenged and encouraged.

THE ISSUE: Relationships

Betrayed!

HELPING KIDS DEAL WITH REJECTION FROM THE PEOPLE THEY LOVE

by Jennifer Cortell

THE POINT:

God is love.

■ Betrayal has very little shock value for this generation. It's as commonplace as compact discs and mosh pits. For many kids today, betrayal characterizes their parents' wedding vows. It's part of their curriculum at school; it defines the headlines and evening news. Betrayal is not only accepted—it's expected. ■ At the heart of such acceptance lies the belief that nothing is absolute. No vow, no law, no promise can be trusted. Relationships are betrayed at the earliest convenience. Repeatedly, kids see that something called "love" lasts just as long as it's ... permanence. But deep inside, they hunger to see a

The Study
AT A GLANCE

SECTION	MINUTES	WHAT STUDENTS WILL DO	SUPPLIES
Discussion Starter	up to 5	JUMP-START—Identify some of the most common themes in today's movies.	Newsprint, marker
Investigation of Betrayal	12 to 15	REALITY CHECK—Form groups to compare anonymous, real-life stories of betrayal with experiences in their own lives.	"Profiles of Betrayal" handouts (p. 20), highlighter pens, newsprint, marker, tape
	3 to 5	WHO BETRAYED WHOM?—Guess the identities of the people profiled in the handouts.	Paper, tape, pen
Investigation of True Love	15 to 18	SOURCE WORK—Study and discuss God's definition of perfect love.	Bibles, newsprint, marker
	5 to 7	LOVE MESSAGES—Create unique ways to send a "message of love" to the victims of betrayal they've been studying.	Newsprint, markers, tape
Personal Application	10 to 15	SYMBOLIC LOVE—Give a partner a personal symbol of perfect love.	Paper lunch sack, pens, scissors, paper, catalogs

notes:

● **A Relevant Topic**—More than ever before, kids live in the now. What matters to them and what attracts their hearts is what's happening in their world at this moment. For this reason, every Core Belief Bible Study focuses on a particular hot topic that kids care about.

● **A Core Christian Belief**—Group's Core Belief Bible Study Series organizes the wealth of Christian truth and experience into twenty-four Core Christian Belief categories. These twenty-four headings act as umbrellas for a collection of detailed beliefs that define Christianity and set it apart from the world and every other religion. Each book in this series features one Core Christian Belief with lessons suited for junior high or senior high students.

"But," you ask, "won't my kids be bored talking about all these spiritual beliefs?" No way! As a youth leader, you know the value of using hot topics to connect with young people. Ultimately teenagers talk about issues because they're searching for meaning in their lives. They want to find the one equation that will make sense of all the confusing events happening around them. Each Core Belief Bible Study answers that need by connecting a hot topic with a powerful Christian principle. Kids walk away from the study with something more solid than just the shifting ebb and flow of their own opinions. They walk away with a deeper understanding of their Christian faith.

● **The Point**—This simple statement is designed to be the intersection between the Core Christian Belief and the hot topic. Everything in the study ultimately focuses on The Point so that kids study it and allow it time to sink into their hearts.

● **The Study at a Glance**—A quick look at this chart will tell you what kids will do, how long it will take them to do it, and what supplies you'll need to get it done.

● **The Bible Connection**—This is the power base of each study. Whether it's just one verse or several chapters, The Bible Connection provides the vital link between kids' minds and their hearts. The content of each Core Belief Bible Study reflects the belief that the true power of God—the power to expose, heal, and change kids' lives—is contained in his Word.

THE POINT OF *BETRAYED!*:

God is love.

THE BIBLE CONNECTION

1 JOHN 4:7-21   The Apostle John explains the nature and definition of perfect love.

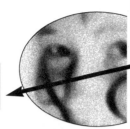

In this study, kids will compare the imperfect love defined in real-life stories of betrayal to God's definition of perfect love.

By making this comparison, kids can discover that God is love and therefore incapable of betraying them. Then they'll be able to recognize the incredible opportunity God off[...]

relationship worthy of their absolute trust.

Explore the verses in The Bible Connection[...]

mation in the Depthfinder boxes throughout t[...]

understanding of how these Scriptures conne[...]

LEADER
TIP

THE STUDY

DISCUSSION STARTER ▼

Jump-Start (up to 5 minutes) As kids arrive, ask them to think[...]
common themes in movies, books, TV show[...]
have kids each contribute ideas for a mast[...]
two other kids in the room and sharing [...]
sider providing copies of People magaz[...]
what's currently showing on television [...]
their suggestions, write their respon[...]
come up with a lot of great ide[...]
ent, look through this list and [...]
ments most of these themes [...]

After kids make several su[...]
responses are connected w[...]

● **Why do you think [...]**

Betrayed!   **17**

LEADER
TIP
for The Study
Because this topic can be so powerful and relevant to kids' lives, your group members may be tempted to get caught up in issues and lose sight of the deeper biblical principle found in The Point. Help your kids grasp The Point by guiding kids to focus on the biblical investigation and discussing how God's truth connects with reality in their lives.

DEPTHFINDER   **UNDERSTANDING INTEGRITY**

Your students may not be entirely familiar with the meaning of integrity, especially as it might apply to God's character in the Trinity. Use these definitions (taken from Webster's II New Riverside Dictionary) and other information to help you guide kids toward a better understanding of how God maintains integrity through the three expressions of the Trinity.

Integrity: 1. Firm adherence to a code or standard of values. 2. The state of being unimpaired. 3. The quality or condition of being undivided.

Synonyms for integrity include probity, completeness, wholeness, soundness, and perfection.

Our word "integrity" comes from the Latin word *integritas*, which means soundness. *Integritas* is also the root of the word "integer," which means "whole or complete," as in a "whole" number.

The Hebrew word that's often translated "integrity" (for example, in Psalm 25:21 [NIV]) is *tam*. It means whole, perfect, sincere, and honest.

CREATIVE GOD-EXPLORATION ▼

Top Hats (18 to 20 minutes) Form three groups, with each trio member from the previous activity going to a different group. Give each group Bibles, paper, and pens, and assign each group a different hat God wears: Father, Son, or Holy Spirit.
[...] their goal is to write one list describing what God does in the [...] God's character

● **Depthfinder Boxes**— These informative sidelights located throughout each study add insight into a particular passage, word, historical fact, or Christian doctrine. Depthfinder boxes also provide insight into teen culture, adolescent development, current events, and philosophy.

● **Leader Tips**— These handy information boxes coach you through the study, offering helpful suggestions on everything from altering activities for different-sized groups to streamlining discussions to using effective discipline techniques.

holy Profiles

Your assigned Bible passage describes how a particular person or group responded when confronted with God's holiness. Use the information in your passage to help your group discuss the questions below. Then use your flashlights to teach the other two groups what you discover.

■ Based on your passage, what does holiness look like?

■ What does holiness sound like?

■ When people see God's holiness, how does it affect them?

■ How is this response to God's holiness like humility?

■ Based on your passage, how would you describe humility?

■ Why is humility an appropriate human response to God's holiness?

■ Based on what you see in your passage, do you think you are a humble person? Why or why not?

■ What's one way you could develop humility in your life this week?

● **Handouts**—Most Core Belief Bible Studies include photocopiable handouts to use with your group. Handouts might take the form of a fun game, a lively discussion starter, or a challenging study page for kids to take home— anything to make your study more meaningful and effective.

The Last Word on Core Belief Bible Studies

Soon after you begin to use Group's Core Belief Bible Study Series, you'll see signs of real growth in your group members. Your kids will gain a deeper understanding of the Bible and of their own Christian faith. They'll see more clearly how a relationship with Jesus affects their daily lives. And they'll grow closer to God.

But that's not all. You'll also see kids grow closer to one another.

That's because this series is founded on the principle that Christian faith grows best in the context of relationship. Each study uses a variety of interactive pairs and small groups and always includes discussion questions that promote deeper relationships. The friendships kids will build through this study series will enable them to grow *together* toward a deeper relationship with God.

hope Through the Storm

by Miriam C. Perry

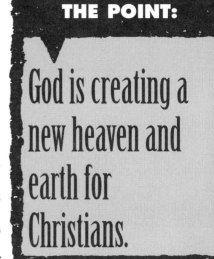

THE POINT:

God is creating a new heaven and earth for Christians.

■ "River at Flood Stage" reads the headline that spells disaster for the small town. Despite safety nets such as levies and dams, individuals and entire cities are often powerless against the unpredictable and uncontrollable forces of nature. ■ Natural disasters leave us wondering what the next day will bring. "Will it happen again?" "Will my home be next?" "Why did God allow this to happen?" Your kids may see these "acts of God" and think that God is acting mean and uncaring. ■ Kids need to know that despite the seemingly indiscriminate destruction of nature, God cares for them and loves them as individuals. God's love isn't suspended or withdrawn during a natural disaster. He is ready and able to provide comfort and hope in the midst of chaos and fear. ■

This study will help kids see what role God plays in natural disasters. It will remind them of the hope we have of a new heaven and earth that is free of pain and disaster.

"Why did God allow this to happen?"

The Study
AT A GLANCE

SECTION	MINUTES	WHAT STUDENTS WILL DO	SUPPLIES
Creative Opener	10 to 15	DISASTER AREA—Create areas representing natural disasters.	Various art supplies, newspaper articles
Bible Learning Experience	10 to 15	WORLD VISION—Investigate the predominate locations of natural disasters around the world, and discuss Romans 8:18-23.	Bibles, "World Map" handouts (p. 24), "Disasters" handouts (p. 23), colored markers
	10 to 15	JARS OF JELLY BEANS—Record and present Scripture passages about the Last Days.	Bibles, red and white jelly beans, jars, paper, pencils
Closing Clean Up	10 to 15	GOD'S FUTURE WORLD—Modify "disaster areas" to look like the new heaven and earth.	Bibles, art supplies from "Disaster Area" activity

notes:

THE POINT OF "HOPE THROUGH THE STORM":

God is creating a new heaven and earth for Christians.

THE BIBLE CONNECTION

MATTHEW 24:4-14, 29-44	Jesus tells his disciples of events that will occur before he returns.
ROMANS 8:18-23	Paul explains the effect sin has on creation.
2 PETER 3:3-13	Peter reminds us that Jesus has promised to bring a new heaven and earth.
REVELATION 6:12-14; 21:1-27	John relays a vision he saw concerning Jesus' return.

I n this study, students will create disaster areas and show how disasters affect the entire world. They'll explore what the Bible says will happen before Jesus returns and modify the disaster areas to show what the new heaven and new earth may look like.

Through this experience, kids can discover the cause of disasters and find hope in God's promise of a new heaven and earth for Christians.

Explore the verses in The Bible Connection, then examine the information in the Depthfinder Boxes throughout the study to gain a deeper understanding of how these Scriptures connect with your young people.

BEFORE THE STUDY

For the "Disaster Area" activity, collect one newspaper or magazine article about each of the following natural disasters: earthquakes, floods, hurricanes, tornadoes, and volcanoes.

LEADER TIP

for The Study

Because this topic can be so powerful and relevant to kids' lives, your group members may be tempted to get caught up in issues and lose sight of the deeper biblical principle found in The Point. Help your kids grasp The Point by guiding kids to focus on the biblical investigation and discussing how God's truth connects with reality in their lives.

THE STUDY

CREATIVE OPENER ▼

LEADER TIP for Disaster Area

If you have difficulty finding articles, provide kids with photos and descriptions of the disasters from an encyclopedia.

Disaster Area (10 to 15 minutes)

Before kids arrive, set out various art supplies such as newsprint, construction paper, foil, tape, and yarn. As kids arrive, have them form five groups. Explain that kids will be turning the room into a disaster area.

Assign one of the following natural disasters to each group without letting kids know what disasters have been assigned to the other groups: earthquakes, floods, hurricanes, tornadoes, and volcanoes. Give each group the newspaper article that corresponds to its assigned disaster from the articles you collected before the study. Have groups refer to their articles for examples of the damage their disasters can cause.

Have each group go to a different area of the room and use the supplies you provided to make the area look like it was hit by the disaster. For example, the "tornado" group could create a representation of a piece of wood stuck in the middle of a chair and could overturn tables in its area.

Give kids about ten minutes to create their disaster areas. Then have groups visit the other areas and attempt to determine what happened. After all the types of disasters have been revealed, have groups discuss the following questions:

● **Which of the disasters do you think would be the most awful to encounter? Why?**

● **How would you feel if your group's disaster hit your community? your home?**

● **In what way does this room accurately represent the emotions that surround a natural disaster? inaccurately?**

● **Have you ever had a natural disaster affect your life? If so, what happened?**

Have kids form pairs and say: **Tell each other one reason why you would want to be with your partner should a disaster really occur. For example, you could say, "I would be glad to have you with me, Bill, because I know you can think calmly even when a lot of things are going on around you."**

LEADER TIP for The Study

Whenever groups discuss a list of questions, write the questions on newsprint, and tape the newsprint to the wall so groups can discuss the questions at their own pace.

When kids finish, say: **Natural disasters can cause serious physical and emotional pain. But God's original plan didn't include disasters. They're a result of sin entering the world. Sin corrupted everything God created, including the forces of nature. Fortunately, it won't always be this way for us. When Jesus returns, God will replace everything that is old and corrupt. In fact, <u>God is creating a new heaven and earth for Christians.</u>**

DEPTH FINDER — DOES GOD CAUSE DISASTERS?

In Lamentations 3:37-38, Jeremiah asks "Who can speak and have it happen if the Lord has not decreed it? Is it not from the mouth of the Most High that both calamities and good things come?" Psalm 147:17 makes it clear that natural disasters are not beyond God's control as it explains that God "hurls down his hail like pebbles." So how could a good and loving God create disasters that bring suffering, pain, and death?

The Quest Study Bible (Zondervan) explains that "All of this world's suffering can be traced back to one tragic event—the disobedience of Adam and Eve (Gen. 3:6-7). Consequently, sin and its result—suffering and evil—entered the world. But God's hands were not tied as a result. In working out his purposes, God often uses suffering to discipline us."

God is working with a world that is different from his original plan. The introduction of sin into creation corrupted nature—but it did not take away God's control. All of the disasters we encounter are a result of a fallen world. Many of the disasters are nothing but the natural progressions of a world poisoned by sin.

But God can use disasters to accomplish his purposes. He can punish, discipline, and even show his power and glory through the forces of nature. These applications of disaster are sometimes necessary methods of helping fallen people turn their hearts and focus back to a good and loving God.

BIBLE LEARNING EXPERIENCE ▼

World Vision

(10 to 15 minutes) Have kids get back in the five groups from the first activity, and form one large circle while staying with their group members. Give each group a "World Map" handout (p. 24), a "Disasters" handout (p. 23), and a colored marker. Make sure each group has a different color of marker. Check to make sure each group remembers which natural disaster it represents.

Say: **On your "World Map" handout, use your colored marker to show each location your natural disaster affects. Refer to your "Disasters" handout as a reference.**

When groups finish, have each group pass its "World Map" handout to the group on the right. Have kids mark the locations of their disasters on the handouts they just received. Continue this process until all five groups have marked all of the handouts.

Have groups discuss the following questions:

● **How did you feel as you saw more and more disasters marked on the page?**

● **By looking at your maps, can you see any patterns or reasoning as to why natural disasters occur?**

● **Does God allow natural disasters to happen? Explain.**

● **Does God cause natural disasters? Explain.**

● **Does looking at your map make you think that nature is in or out of God's control?**

Have kids come together and report what they learned to the rest of the class. Then have kids open their Bibles to Romans 8:18-23. Ask:

LEADER TIP
for World Vision

Bring a globe, atlas, or wall map of the world to help kids find the countries on their handouts.

● **According to Romans 8:18-23, what is the cause of natural disasters?**
● **What hope do these verses offer concerning natural disasters?**

● **How does the fact that <u>God is creating a new heaven and earth for Christians</u> affect your view of natural disasters?**

With your kids, take turns praying aloud. Encourage kids to focus on those who suffer from disasters. Ask kids to take turns praying aloud if they feel comfortable doing so.

LEADER TIP
for Jars of Jelly Beans

After the activity, allow groups to share the candy.

Jars of Jelly Beans (10 to 15 minutes)

Have kids return to the five disaster groups. Give each group fifteen red jelly beans, fifteen white jelly beans, and a small jar.

Assign each group one of the following Scripture passages:
● Matthew 24:4-14
● Matthew 24:29-44
● 2 Peter 3:3-13
● Revelation 6:12-14
● Revelation 21:1-7

Say: **Each candy represents what God has outlined for our world concerning natural disasters and the events surrounding the Last**

Days. Read your assigned passage. Identify the disasters and the words of hope that serve as reminders that <u>God is creating a new heaven and earth for Christians.</u>

LEADER TIP
for Jars of Jelly Beans

If jelly beans aren't available, provide other objects that are similar in size but can be easily differentiated. For example, nickels and pennies will work.

Have each group appoint a reader, a recorder, a reporter, and a leader. Say: **The reader will read the passage aloud to his or her group. Whenever the reader mentions any destruction or disaster, the recorder will write down the type of disaster, and the reporter will drop a red jelly bean into the group's jar. Whenever the reader mentions any indication of hope, the reporter will drop a white jelly bean into the jar. The leader will help the group get started and will help keep things moving along. When you're done with your passage, discuss the following questions:**

● **What effect will the events you read about have on the earth and its life forms?**

● **What does the amount of each color of jelly beans in your jar tell you about the Last Days?**

● **What are your feelings about the Last Days?**

● **Does the fact that <u>God is creating a new heaven and earth for Christians</u> give you hope for today? for your future?**

● **Did your Bible passage change the way you think or feel about disasters? Why or why not?**

● **How can a disaster be used by God for good?**

Have each reporter take out each piece of candy from the jar and tell the entire group the hope or disaster that the piece represents. Then ask:

● **Are you looking forward to or dreading Christ's return? Explain.**

Say: **Pain, suffering, and disasters are a result of sin entering the world. Creation was corrupted when Adam and Eve first sinned** against God. Despite the terror and harm of disasters, God has given us hope. When God makes everything right again—when he brings a new heaven and earth for Christians—pain, suffering, and disasters will no longer exist. We may have to endure some difficult circumstances until that day, but his return is the beginning of an incredible and wonderful eternity for Christians.

CLOSING CLEAN UP ▼

God's Future World
(10 to 15 minutes)
Say: **God is creating a new heaven and earth for Christians.** **It will be an exciting new world, and Christians will be a part of it. Let's go back to the disaster areas we created in this room as the class began. Adjust your area to show what you think the new heaven and earth will look like.**

Direct kids to the supplies you provided for the "Disaster Area" activity. Say: **Use the supplies I've provided to demonstrate the difference. Read Revelation 21:1-27 for some ideas.**

When kids finish, commend them for a job well done and say: **God is creating a new heaven and earth for Christians.** **God has promised that this new earth will be free of the pain, confusion, and suffering of disasters of any kind. Let's take a minute to celebrate the hope we have.**

Have kids get in groups of four and pray. Encourage kids to thank God for all the things they are hopeful about concerning the Last Days and their immediate future.

DEPTHFINDER — UNDERSTANDING THE LAST DAYS

"I'm premillennial and partial-rapture." "I'm either pre-tribulation or post-trib, but I'm certain that I'm not amillennial." "I'm somewhere between midtribulation and post-trib, and I'm leaning more towards postmillennial."

The timing and method of Jesus' return has sparked considerable controversy. We want to know when and how Jesus will return because we want to be ready for it. Regardless of your theory of Jesus' method and timing in his return, you can prepare for it right now. The preparation that Jesus spoke of in Matthew 24 is less concerned with setting dates and interpreting current events than it is with the preparation of our hearts and minds.

The first step of the preparation is, of course, to make Jesus the Lord of our lives. Ask your kids, "Is Jesus your Lord or just your religion?" Encourage kids to ask Jesus to become their Lord if he isn't already.

The next step is concerned with making choices that please God. Challenge kids to repent for their sin, to love others, and to work on building the sort of character they'd be proud to show Jesus when they meet him face to face.

Another step in the preparation is to share the message with others. The Gospel can be shared through acts of service, invitations to church, or simply telling others about Jesus. Ask your students to help others begin to prepare for Christ's return by encouraging their friends to take the first and most important step of preparation.

Challenging your kids to take these steps seriously will help them prepare for Christ's return—whether they see him after a post-tribulation rapture, a pre-tribulation rapture, or without going through a tribulation or a rapture at all.

"Then I saw a new heaven and a new earth, for the first heaven and the first earth had passed away, and there was no longer any sea." —Revelation 21:1

disasters

EARTHQUAKES

An earthquake is the vibration or movement of the earth's surface caused by the abrupt movement or displacement of the rock masses within the earth's crust. Earthquakes most frequently occur in India and along the rim of the Pacific Ocean: Alaska, California, Chile, Japan, and Mexico.

FLOODS

A flood is a great overflowing of water over land not usually submerged. Major floods have occurred in Brazil, China, India, the Philippine Islands, and the United States.

HURRICANES

A hurricane is a violent, tropical, cyclonic storm of the western North Atlantic having high wind speeds. Hurricanes occur in the Caribbean Islands; Florida, Texas, and other Gulf of Mexico states; and Southeastern coastal states of the United States.

TORNADOES

A tornado is a localized, violently destructive windstorm occurring over land characterized by a long, funnel-like cloud. Tornadoes occur most frequently in the Midwestern United States and the western coast of Africa, China, and India.

VOLCANOES

A volcano is a mountain formed by the magma coming from a vent or an opening in the earth's crust, through which ash and lava escape to the surface. Volcanoes exist in Hawaii, Italy, Japan, Washington state, the Philippine Islands, the Caribbean Islands, and many other places around the world.

Definitions taken from The Random House College Dictionary, Revised Edition, Jess Stein, editor.
Locations of disasters taken from the Atlas of the Environment, Geoffrey Lean, editor.

WORLD Map

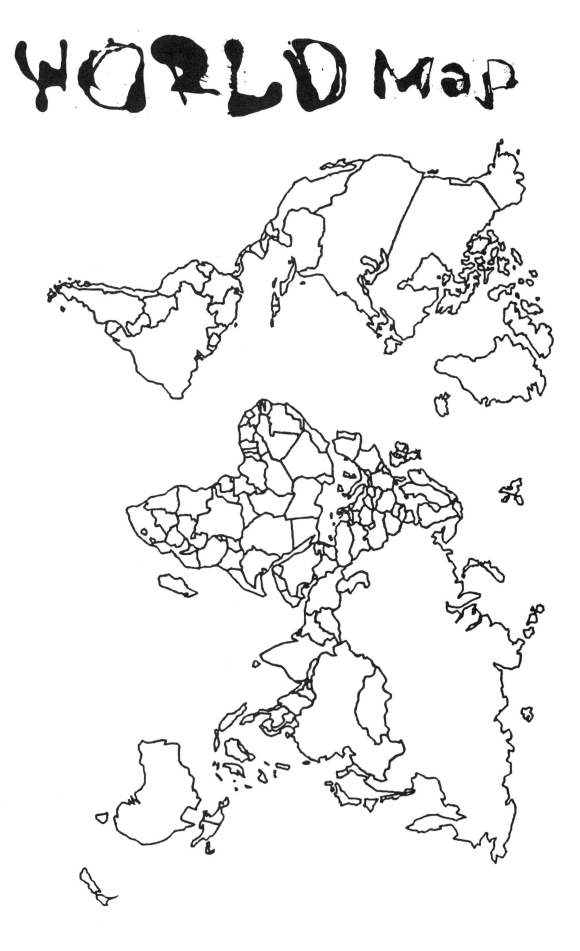

A Look at Our @ Future

by Rick Chromey

THE POINT:

Christ will return someday to judge the world.

■ The quest to understand the Last Days can be a consuming passion. ■ Junior highers especially can be drawn into speculations about future things. They're driven by the process of becoming adults—learning a trade, finding a mate, becoming an autonomous individual. Who can't remember the teenage angst and fear surrounding the question: "What if the world ends before I get to...?" ■ It's within such a context that adolescents need reassurance. Jesus will most certainly return as promised. A faith too focused upon the future and dwell in present hope rather than the future event. A faith too focused upon the future and its fears may rob a person of the beauty and blessings of the present. ■ This study will help junior high kids understand that God is in control of the future—regardless of their understanding of it. It will encourage kids to commit to faithful Christian lives in the present—dominated by holiness, purity, and peace with God.

The Study
AT A GLANCE

SECTION	MINUTES	WHAT STUDENTS WILL DO	SUPPLIES
Creative Opener	10 to 15	PROGNOSTICATION—"Prophesy" about present situations, and discuss man's inability to know everything.	Bibles, pencils, paper
Bible Discovery	10 to 15	BLIND GUIDES—Search for objects while other students verbally lead or mislead them.	Bibles, blindfolds, various objects, tape
	15 to 20	ACCURACY CHECK—Check the accuracy of Messianic prophecies.	Bibles, paper, pencils, "Accuracy Check" handouts (p. 33)
Life Change	5 to 10	THE HEAT IS ON—Prepare for Jesus' return.	Bibles, index cards, pencils

notes:

Christ will return someday to judge the world.

THE BIBLE CONNECTION

PSALM 16:10; ISAIAH 7:14; MICAH 5:2; ZECHARIAH 9:9	These passages prophesy about the coming Messiah.
MATTHEW 2:1; 21:6-9; MARK 16:4-6; LUKE 1:26-35	These passages describe the fulfillment of a few Old Testament prophecies.
MATTHEW 24:36; 2 PETER 3:3-11	These passages address events surrounding Jesus' second coming.
2 PETER 1:19-21; 1 JOHN 4:1-3	These passages show the difference between false and genuine prophecy.

I n this study, kids will attempt to prophesy about the lives of their friends, look for hidden objects, share messages about Christ's return, and make a commitment regarding their preparation for his return.

Through this experience, kids can learn that God knows the future and they can trust his Word about future matters. They can discover that living as victorious, holy Christians in the present is more advantageous than fearing and guessing about what the future holds.

Explore the verses in The Bible Connection, then examine the information in the Depthfinder boxes throughout the study to gain a deeper understanding of how these Scriptures connect with your young people.

BEFORE THE STUDY

For the "Blind Guides" activity, write each of the following sections of Matthew 24:36 on a separate sheet of paper:
● No one knows about
● that day or hour,
● not even the angels in heaven,
● nor the Son,
● but only the Father.

Tape each sheet on a separate ordinary object, such as an eraser or a book, and keep the objects out of sight until the activity.

LEADER TIP for The Study

Because this topic can be so powerful and relevant to kids' lives, your group members may be tempted to get caught up in issues and lose sight of the deeper biblical principle found in The Point. Help your kids grasp The Point by guiding kids to focus on the biblical investigation and discussing how God's truth connects with reality in their lives.

THE STUDY

CREATIVE OPENER ▼

Prognostication (10 to 15 minutes)

Have kids form pairs and sit back-to-back. Give every student a pencil and a sheet of paper. Say: **Without talking to your partner, I'd like you to make a few guesses about what he or she is like and what he or she will become. Write your answers to each of the following questions on the sheet of paper I've given you.** Ask each of the following questions while allowing time for students to write after each one:

1. **What is your partner's favorite color?**
2. **What is the name of your partner's grandmother?**
3. **What did your partner do at 7:30 last night?**
4. **What will your partner do after this meeting is over?**
5. **What will your partner's career be in fifteen years?**

Say: **Flip your sheet of paper over and write down a description of what your partner looks like without looking at him or her. Try to make it as detailed as possible, but avoid writing anything down that may offend or hurt your partner.**

Give kids about a minute to work. Have partners compare answers. Then have each pair get together with another pair to form groups of four. Have groups discuss:

● **How accurate were your answers to the questions?**

● **Why were you able to guess more accurately on certain questions?**

● **Is it easier to make believable predictions about the future or to tell of things that currently exist or have already happened? Explain.**

● **Read 2 Peter 1:19-21. What's the difference between the predictions you made and prophecy in the Bible?**

● **Can people today be directed by God to prophesy? Why or why not?**

Give groups a few minutes to share what they discovered. Then say: **A prediction is different from a prophecy. A prediction takes facts and probabilities into account and produces a best guess. A prediction may or may not come true based on the variables involved. Prophecy is a message given by God. A prophecy doesn't take circumstances or probabilities into account but is guaranteed to happen because it comes from the all-knowing God.** Ask:

● **What are some predictions you've heard about our country? our community? about Jesus' return?**

● **What are some prophecies you're aware of about our world? about Jesus' return?**

DEPTH FINDER — WHAT IS A CULT?

Many false prophets exist who lead their followers into cults. However, the term "cult" is often misapplied in contemporary Christianity. Josh McDowell and Don Stewart, in their book *Understanding the Cults*, provide several characteristics of cults:

- **New Truth.** Cults tend to suggest God has revealed something special only to them.
- **New Interpretations of Scripture.** Some cults believe they alone have the key to interpreting the mysteries of the Bible.
- **A Non-Biblical Source of Authority.** Some cults have sacred writings or a source of authority that supersedes the Bible.
- **Another Jesus.** One characteristic of all cults is false teaching about Jesus Christ.
- **Double-Talk.** Some cultic groups say one thing publicly but really believe something totally different.
- **Non-Biblical Teaching on the Nature of God.** All non-Christian cults have an inadequate view or state outright denial of the Holy Trinity.
- **Changing Theology.** Cult doctrines are continually in a state of flux and have no sure foundation on which to anchor their hope.
- **Strong Leadership.** Cults are usually characterized by central leader figures who consider themselves messengers of God with unique access to the Almighty.
- **Salvation by Works.** One teaching that is totally absent from cults is the gospel of the grace of God.
- **False Prophecy.** Cult leaders often make bold predictions of future events.

The Bible gives some definite prophecies about our world. One clear prophecy is that <u>Christ will return someday to judge the world.</u> The Bible doesn't predict when his return will occur, but we can be certain that he will return.

BIBLE DISCOVERY ▼

Blind Guides

(10 to 15 minutes)
Have kids put on blindfolds. Quietly set out the objects with the phrases from Matthew 24:36 that you prepared before the study.

Say: **Five objects are placed around the room that display portions of a Scripture verse. The objects would be in plain view if you weren't blindfolded. Your job is to find these objects without removing your blindfolds. Once all the objects have been discovered, I'd like you to put the Scripture statements in order while you keep your blindfolds on.**

Tell kids to begin the search. After a minute, have two students remove their blindfolds. Instruct one of the kids without blindfolds to verbally direct the others toward the objects. Instruct the other student without a blindfold to verbally direct others away from the objects.

Say: **Two of your peers are now able to see all the objects. They'll give you guidance on finding the objects and putting them in the correct order.**

After all the objects have been found and the Scriptures have been placed in the proper order, have everyone remove their blindfolds and form groups of four. Have groups discuss:

● **What were you thinking and feeling as we played this game?**

● **How did you decide whose advice to follow?**

● **How can you know whose advice you can follow concerning the Last Days?**

● **Read 1 John 4:1-3. What should be our standard for recognizing false prophets?**

● **What does it mean to "test the spirits"?**

● **Are there false prophets today? If so, what are they like?**

● **Why do false prophets seem so concerned with future events?**

Say: **It's difficult to know what voices to believe concerning the Last Days. Fortunately, the Bible has given us information regarding the most important facts. We know that <u>Christ will return someday to judge the world.</u> We also know that no one, except the Father, knows when that will happen. The Bible also makes it clear that we should prepare for Jesus' return by growing in character, faith, and love.**

Accuracy Check (15 to 20 minutes)

Ask:

● **Are you willing to stake the way you live your life on the prophecies the Bible gives about the Last Days? Why or why not?**

● **Why should or shouldn't we trust the prophecies in the Bible about the future?**

DEPTHFINDER

WHEN JESUS RETURNS

Date-setting is a popular pastime.

And it's easy to get caught up in trying to determine just *when* Jesus might return. Knowing the exact date would provide a sense of security from God's judgment. After all, if we think Jesus won't return for another three, forty, or three hundred years, why not "live it up" a bit? And if we believe he'll return tonight, why not sell the house, alter our plans, or "get right with God"?

The problem with date-setting is that the Bible says no one but God knows the date (Matthew 24:36).

The biblical record is very clear on *how* Jesus will return. Suddenly and unexpectedly, Jesus will return in great glory. Jesus will arrive for his own people, his church and "bride." He will judge the world, oversee its destruction, and conquer death. As believers, we will be with the Lord forever.

The challenge as a Christian isn't to live right on the night of Christ's return, but to live right daily—until he comes. As Peter asks, rhetorically, "What kind of people ought you to be?" The answer is obvious. We should be pure and holy—making every effort to serve God.

Have kids form four groups, and give each group an "Accuracy Check" handout (p. 33), paper, and pencils.

Say: **Believing that <u>Christ will return someday to judge the world</u> affects everything we do and say. If we don't believe he'll return, there is no need to obey his commands. If we do believe he will return, his commands are vitally important. As you work on this handout, think about reasons why we should or shouldn't believe the prophecies in the Bible about the Last Days.**

Assign one prophecy from the handout to each group, and instruct kids to follow the directions on the handouts.

When kids finish, have each group give a brief description of the prophecy it looked at and how the prophecy was fulfilled. Ask:

● **Does the handout help you trust the prophecies in the Bible? Why or why not?**

● **Do you believe the prophecies in the Bible about the Last Days are accurate? Why or why not?**

Say: **There are more than forty prophecies throughout the Old Testament that were specifically fulfilled by the life, death, and resurrection of Jesus. We can trust *all* the prophecies in the Bible because the Bible has demonstrated a perfect track record so far. Let's look at one of those prophecies right now.**

The Heat Is On (5 to 10 minutes)

Have kids get in pairs and read 2 Peter 3:3-11. Have pairs discuss the following questions:

● **What types of things does Peter say people will do and say about Christians who believe in Jesus' return?**

● **Have such situations ever occurred in your life? Explain.**

● **When Peter reminds his readers that people forget "what happened long ago," what event is he speaking about?**

● **Why do you think Peter referred to this event?**

● **Are you looking forward to or dreading Jesus' return? Explain.**

While kids talk, give each student an index card and a pencil. Have students write the following statement at the top of their cards:

"If I knew for sure that Jesus would return to judge me by tomorrow noon, I would make the following specific life changes now…"

Instruct kids to complete the statement on their index cards and discuss the answers with their partners. Then have partners pray for each other—asking God to help them make the life changes as quickly as possible.

When kids finish praying, have partners share one quality they see in each other that shows evidence that they're getting ready for Christ's judgment. For example, a student could say, "Devon, I can tell you are getting ready for Christ's return because of the way you serve others."

"Above all, you must understand that no prophecy of Scripture came about by the prophet's own interpretation. For prophecy never had its origin in the will of man, but men spoke from God as they were carried along by the Holy Spirit."—2 Peter 1:20-21

Accuracy Check

Read the prophecy that has been assigned to your group, and compare it to the passage that describes its fulfillment. Then discuss the questions at the bottom of the handout.

	Fulfillment	
Prophecy		**Approximate amount of time before prophecy was fulfilled**
1 Zechariah 9:9	Matthew 21:6-9	520 years
2 Isaiah 7:14	Luke 1:26-35	700 years
3 Micah 5:2	Matthew 2:1	725 years
4 Psalm 16:10	Mark 16:4-6	1,000 years

● Do you think the prophets in the Bible knew they were prophesying about the Messiah? Why or why not?

● What does the comparison of the two passages say about the accuracy of biblical prophecy?

● What does the duration of time between the prophecy and the fulfillment say about prophecies that haven't been fulfilled yet?

Beyond the Door

Helping Kids Prepare for Eternity

by Pamela T. Campbell

■ According to present statistics, 100 percent of your students will die someday. There may be a few exceptions. Some or all of your kids may still be alive when Jesus returns. But regardless of how they get there, all of your kids will enter into eternity one day. ■ This may not come as welcome news to junior high kids. Their whole lives are just ahead of them—waiting to be experienced and enjoyed. It's natural for your kids to be a little afraid of death, because death is the end of the life they know and the future they're looking forward to. ■ The Bible makes it clear that *the* last day will be frightening and terrible. But Christians don't have to dread or fear the beginning of eternity. Death and Christ's return mark the beginning of real life for Christians. Eternity with God is our real future. ■ This study will help your kids see that they can look forward to life after death as they prepare for it daily.

THE POINT:

Because of Christ, there is life in heaven after death.

The Study
AT A GLANCE

SECTION	MINUTES	WHAT STUDENTS WILL DO	SUPPLIES
Getting Started	15 to 20	TENTMATES—Set up tents, and compare the shelters with our earthly bodies.	Bible, bedsheets, masking tape, balls
Bible Study	10 to 15	PICTURE THIS—Create a mural that symbolizes eternal life.	Bibles, "On Your Last Day" handouts (p. 45), colored markers, bedsheet from "Tentmates" activity
Case Studies	15 to 20	LIFE WORTH LIVING—Discuss examples of suffering, and debate why certain people should go on living.	Bibles
Creative Closing	5 to 10	EPITAPHS—Write epitaphs that serve as reminders of their commitment to live lives that please God, then pray about the commitment.	Paper, pencils

notes:

Because of Christ, there is life in heaven after death.

THE BIBLE CONNECTION

ISAIAH 11:6-9; 25:6-8; MICAH 4:1-4; 1 CORINTHIANS 15:42-44; 2 CORINTHIANS 5:1-5; REVELATION 21:3-4	These passages describe what life after death will be like for Christians.
 PHILIPPIANS 1:20-26	This passage demonstrates the benefits of living and dying as a Christian.

I n this study, students will build tents and compare the shelters with earthly bodies, create murals symbolizing eternal life, debate the necessity of enduring suffering, and write epitaphs that describe what they'd like to be remembered for.

Through this experience, kids can discover that because of Christ, there is life in heaven after death for Christians.

Explore the verses in The Bible Connection, then examine the information in the Depthfinder boxes throughout the study to gain a deeper understanding of how these Scriptures connect with your students.

THE STUDY

GETTING STARTED ▼

Tentmates (15 to 20 minutes) Have kids form teams of four to six. Give each team a bedsheet, and place a few roles of masking tape in the middle of the

room. Instruct the teams to each set up a tent of their own design using the sheets and masking tape. Tell groups that they'll have about seven minutes to create a tent that's as sturdy as possible. Point to one side of the room, and instruct all of the groups to build the tents there.

After about seven minutes, have kids come back together. Read 2 Corinthians 5:1-5 aloud. Ask:
- **How are the tents you created like our earthly bodies?**
- **How are they different?**
- **How sturdy are your tents?**
- **How sturdy are our earthly bodies?**

Have kids stand on one side of the room. Set out an assortment of balls of different sizes. Have teams throw the balls at each other's tents to try to collapse the tents. Instruct all of the kids to stay on one side of the room. Make sure you remove breakables, and instruct kids to refrain from throwing the balls in any way that will cause injury or damage.

After about three minutes, read 2 Corinthians 5:1-5 again, and have kids return to their groups to discuss these questions:
- **What will happen to us when our earthly tents are destroyed?**
- **What unpredictable things in life could destroy our earthly tents?**
- **How can we protect our earthly tents from collapsing?**

Say: **Your days on earth are numbered. Your earthly tent may last a few years more or less than the tents of others, but it will eventually collapse.** Ask:
- **Are you afraid of death? Why or why not?**
- **What other feelings do you have about death?**

Say: **It's natural to be a little afraid of death. We don't know what death feels like, and we can't know exactly what happens when we die. But we can be certain that <u>because of Christ, there is life in heaven after death.</u> If you are a Christian, the end of this life marks the beginning of eternal life in heaven.**

BIBLE STUDY ▼

LEADER TIP
for Picture This

Put newspaper or plastic under the sheet to prevent the markers from bleeding onto your carpet.

Picture This (10 to 15 minutes)
Have kids form four groups. Give each group a copy of the "On Your Last Day" handout (p. 45), and assign one section of the handout to each group.

Say: **Not everyone is going to die. Some people will be alive when Jesus returns. But both Christians who die and Christians who are alive during Jesus' second coming will witness significant changes as they enter eternity. With your group, go through your section of the handout to see what those changes will be.**

While kids work, set colored markers in the middle of the room. Take one of the bedsheets from the first activity and spread it out in the middle of the room.

When kids finish their handouts, say: **We're going to create a mural on this sheet that shows what life after death will be like**

DEPTHFINDER   TWO KINDS OF DEATH

This study may bring up uncomfortable feelings for some of your students who have lost a loved one. Encourage those students that grieving is part of the natural process necessary for dealing with loss. *Josh McDowell's Handbook on Counseling Youth* by Josh McDowell and Bob Hostetler explains Elizabeth Kubler-Ross' five stages of grief:

1. Denial—The person may refuse to believe that the death has occurred. This stage may vary in length, with some people staying in denial longer than others. It is a temporary stage, but may surface again at any time.

2. Anger—The youth may question why death has occurred. When the answer is not apparent, he or she may lash out in anger at the seeming unfairness of it all.

3. Bargaining—This is usually an attempt to postpone an imminent death or "cut a deal" that will lessen the pain of grief or the reality of separation. The bargaining is usually done in secrecy, with God.

4. Depression—Depression often sets in when the person faces the reality of the death.

5. Acceptance—After working through the feelings and conflicts that have arisen, the person may now be ready to accept the fact of the death.

Assure your students that it's normal to go through all of these stages. Encourage your kids that it's also normal to speak to a counselor if they feel that they'd like help through any or all of the stages.

for Christians. With your group, create a picture of life after death according to the passage your group investigated. Use the markers to draw pictures and write descriptions on the sheet.

When kids finish, have groups use the pictures they created to teach the other groups about the passages they discussed. Then ask:

● **What does the mural we created say about what life after death will be like for Christians?**

● **Does this mural help relieve some of the fears you have about death? Explain.**

Then say: **Because of Christ, there is life in heaven after death.** The certainty of death and our confidence in Christ's return give us license to live for and with God without reservation. The problems and struggles of this world become much less important when we remember that we will spend eternity with Jesus after we die. We don't have to be afraid because God gave us his word.

CASE STUDIES ▼

Life Worth Living
(15 to 20 minutes)
Ask a volunteer to read Revelation 21:3-4 aloud. Ask:

● **What hope does this verse give about death?**

● **What part of eternal life do you look forward to the most? the least?**

DEPTH FINDER
CRIES FOR HELP

The common link among students (and adults) who commit suicide is the belief that killing themselves is the only solution to a set of overwhelming and unbearable feelings. Tragically, this intense emotional distress prevents children and teens from perceiving the alternative solutions that are always available.

Although depression is probably the largest single risk factor for suicide in adolescents, difficulties in family relationships make a significant independent contribution to this risk. Regardless of the nature of the crisis, if a student feels overwhelmed, there is danger that suicide will become an attractive solution.

Note any suicidal statements made by your students during the study. Listen for any "cries for help" that might be communicated during this debate.

Josh McDowell's Handbook on Counseling Youth by Josh McDowell and Bob Hostetler offers some signs that may alert you to a possible risk for a suicide attempt:

- Previous suicide attempts
- Threats of suicide
- Talking about death
- Preparation for death (cleaning out locker, giving away possessions, etc.)
- Moodiness
- Withdrawal
- Somatic complaints (sleeplessness, sleeping all the time)
- Fatigue
- Increased risk-taking
- Drafting of a suicide note

Talk with your pastor or a qualified counselor before the study regarding your responsibilities concerning students contemplating suicide. McDowell cautions: "If a youth has attempted suicide (or is seriously contemplating or threatening an attempt), your responsibility is both urgent and simple: get the young person immediately to a mental health hospital or emergency room; a professional evaluation is absolutely necessary. If you fail to do so and the young person attempts to take his or her life, you may be considered legally responsible."

For information on programs designed to prevent youth suicide, write or call:

The American Association of Suicidology
4201 Connecticut Avenue NW Suite 310
Washington, DC 20008 USA
(202) 237-2280.

● **Why does God let us grow through struggles on earth when we would be much happier just going to heaven?**

Have kids form two debate teams. Say: **I'm going to give you a few situations. For each situation, I'd like one group to come up with reasons each of the following people should want to be with the Lord rather than remain in their earthly bodies. The other group will come up with reasons the following people should want to remain in their earthly bodies rather than going to their eternal home.**

Assign one role to each group. Instruct both groups to use Philippians 1:20-26 as a basis for at least one of the reasons they give for each situation. Give teams a minute to come up with their reasons after you list each of the following circumstances. Then give each team

DEPTH FINDER

WHEN DEATH COMES UNEXPECTEDLY

Children who live with violence sometimes repress their feelings. This defense mechanism can interfere with their ability to empathize and be sensitive to others' loss and grief. Help your students express their feelings and develop better empathic skills as you discuss the following questions:

● How would you handle the unexpected death of a friend or family member? Would you respond in any of the following ways—get angry, withdraw, call a friend, stay busy, keep everything inside, pretend nothing happened, toughen up, cry uncontrollably, get depressed? Why would you respond in that way?

● What do you think would be the most helpful thing to do for someone who is grieving a death? Would you send flowers or a card? Call the person? Hug the person? Take some food to the person? Share some Scripture? Be present and listen? Encourage the person? Take the person to a movie or to the mall?

one minute to debate:

● an eighteen-year-old prisoner serving a life sentence

● a fourteen-year-old who is HIV-positive

● a sixteen-year-old paraplegic (a person who can't move his or her lower body)

● a twelve-year-old victim of abuse

Say: **Both teams have done an excellent job in the debate. I'm going to tell you about a few people who probably struggled with a few of the questions you raised during the debate.** Read the following examples to your students:

● *Helen Adams Keller* **was born in Alabama in 1880. She became blind and deaf when she was only nineteen months old. But with the help of her teacher, Anne Sullivan, Keller learned to read Braille and to write. Keller graduated with honors from Radcliffe College and began a life of writing, lecturing, and fundraising on behalf of the handicapped. She was an author, lecturer, and humanitarian who had an international influence on the lives of the handicapped.** (Source: Compton's Living Encyclopedia)

● *Joni Eareckson Tada* **has spent more than thirty years in a wheelchair since a diving accident left her a quadriplegic at age seventeen. During two years of rehabilitation, she spent long months learning how to paint by holding a brush between her teeth. Today, she is an internationally known advocate for the disabled, a radio host, an author, a conference speaker, and an artist. She is the founder and president of JAF Ministries—an organization accelerating Christian ministry for people with disabilities. Joni's role as an advocate for people with disabilities led to a presidential appointment on the National Council on Disability for three and a half years, during which time the Americans with Disabilities Act became law.** (Source: JAF Ministries Home Page)

● *John Perkins* **was nearly beaten to death in a Mississippi jail for leading protest marches and boycotts against discrimination and unjust laws for black Mississippians. His children suffered** the loneliness, cruelty, and emotional stress that accompanied integrating an all-white school in the '60s. Having survived all that, he went on to found Mendenhall Ministries in Mendenhall, Mississippi; Voice of Calvary Ministries in Jackson, Mississippi; Harambee Christian Family Center in Northwest Pasadena, California; and the Christian Community Development Association.

Have kids get in groups of four to discuss:

● **Do you think these heroes ever looked at death as a favorable option? Explain.**

● **Why is it so difficult to see the purpose of suffering when we're in the middle of it?**

● **Do you think all suffering serves a purpose? Why or why not?**

● **What would you tell someone who said that his or her life is no longer worth living?**

Say: **The Bible makes it clear that we all have a purpose while we are alive and we have no right to cut that purpose short. We also know that when Christians die, their struggles and pain will end. Because of Christ, there is life after death. We can look forward to our permanent home, life, and new body in heaven as we struggle and work through the purpose that God has called us to today.**

eagerly expect and hope that I will in no way be ashamed, but will have sufficient courage so that now as always Christ will be exalted in my body, whether by life or by death. For to me, to live is Christ and to die is gain. If I am to go on living in the body, this will mean fruitful labor for me. Yet what shall I choose? I do not know!

—Philippians 1:20-22

Epitaphs (5 to 10 minutes)

Give each student a pencil and a sheet of paper. Say: **We're going to write our own epitaphs. An epitaph is a brief statement that commemorates or summarizes the life of a person who has died. For example, "Hers was a life well-lived," "He was a man of pizazz," or "Here lies Joe who gave his all for what he could not keep." Write a short statement of no more than twenty-five words that demonstrates how you want to be remembered and what you want your life to have accomplished before you die.**

The wolf will live with the lamb, the leopard will lie down with the goat, the calf and the lion and the yearling together; and a little child will lead them. The cow will feed with the bear, their young will lie down together, and the lion will eat straw like the ox. The infant will play near the hole of the cobra, and the young child put his hand into the viper's nest. They will neither harm nor destroy on all my holy mountain, for the earth will be full of the knowledge of the Lord as the waters cover the sea.

—*Isaiah 11:6-9*

Give your students several minutes to write their epitaphs. Then ask volunteers to read their epitaphs aloud. Ask:

- **What do you want to accomplish before you die?**
- **What spiritual goals do you have for your life?**
- **How can you make sure that you are remembered as a person who lived a life that pleased God?**

Have your students take a minute to reflect on this discussion and make any changes in their epitaphs that would reflect how they want to be remembered. Have kids get in pairs and share what things they think have already come true or will come true on their partners' epitaphs.

Say: **You don't have to fear death if you have a relationship with God. <u>Because of Christ, there is life in heaven after death for Christians.</u> A relationship with God comes through believing that Jesus died for our sins and by trusting in him for salvation. We're going to take a minute to pray and think about our relationships with God. If you're not sure you believe in God or if you're not sure that you're a Christian, consider making the choice to begin putting your trust in Jesus. Consider asking Jesus to forgive you for your sins. If you feel confident that you are a Christian, ask God to show you how to live for him.**

Give kids a couple of minutes to pray and reflect. Then pray aloud: **God, thank you for saving us from eternal death through Jesus. Show each one of us how we can live lives that are pleasing to you. Help us to remember that there is life in heaven after death for Christians because of what you've done for us. In Jesus' name, amen.**

After the prayer, tell kids who want to know what it means to be a Christian that you'd be happy to talk with them.

OnYour Last Day

To get a picture of what Christians can expect at the beginning of eternity,
read your assigned passage(s) and answer the questions that follow.

Section One

Isaiah 25:6-8

- What will God do about death?

- What does this passage say about what life after death will be like?

Section Two

Micah 4:1-4

- How will people relate with God?

- What does this passage say about what life after death will be like?

Section Three

Isaiah 11:6-9

- When will the events in this passage take place?

- What does this passage say about what life after death will be like?

Section Four

1 Corinthians 15:42-44

- What will happen to us after we die?

- What does this passage say about what life after death will be like?

GIVE IT AWAY

Helping Kids Invest Their Talents

by Siv M. Ricketts

THE POINT:

Christ could return at any time.

■ "I'm just no good at anything." How often have you heard, felt, or said that? Discovering your talents and how to use them can be a tough process. It may take years, even a lifetime, of fine-tuning and practice before we're really adept at using the gifts God has given us. ■ But that's not an excuse to wait. Growth doesn't occur without practice. And junior high is the *ideal* time to take risks and experiment to help discover and develop new abilities. We must be faithful with what God has given us during the time that he's given us. ■ This study will challenge kids to discover their talents and begin to use them to serve the Lord now, rather than waiting until they feel old enough, good enough, or prepared enough.

The Study
AT A GLANCE

SECTION	MINUTES	WHAT STUDENTS WILL DO	SUPPLIES
Opening Experience	10 to 15	JACKPOT!—Create an ad for a charity, and discuss how they use their money, talents, and time.	Bibles, newsprint, tape, markers
Bible Experience	10 to 15	WHAT TALENTS?—Help each other discover talents and abilities.	Newsprint, tape, colored markers, "Gifted by God" handouts (p. 55), pencils
	15 to 20	THE PARABLE—Investigate the characters in the parable of the talents, then role-play situations to see how the characters would respond.	Bibles
Closing Experience	5 to 10	"WELL DONE..."—Listen to a story about using their gifts, then commit to using their God-given talents.	"Investing Talents" handouts (p. 56), pencils

notes:

THE POINT OF "GIVE IT AWAY":

Christ could return at any time.

THE BIBLE CONNECTION

MATTHEW 25:14-30	This passage tells a parable of three servants who used their master's gifts in different ways.
1 CORINTHIANS 15:58	This passage describes how and why we should serve God.
2 CORINTHIANS 9:7-8	This passage describes how we should view giving.

I n this study, kids will evaluate how they use their money, talents, and time; decide what their talents may be and how they can use them; and examine biblical perspectives on using what God has given them.

By doing this, kids can discover that God has given them specific talents that they can and should use now, since Christ could return at any time.

Explore the verses in The Bible Connection, then examine the information in the Depthfinder boxes throughout the study to gain a deeper understanding of how these Scriptures connect with your young people.

LEADER TIP for The Study

Because this topic can be so powerful and relevant to kids' lives, your group members may be tempted to get caught up in issues and lose sight of the deeper biblical principle found in The Point. Help your kids grasp The Point by guiding kids to focus on the biblical investigation and discussing how God's truth connects with reality in their lives.

THE STUDY

OPENING EXPERIENCE ▼

Jackpot! (10 to 15 minutes) Ask students to form groups of three. Say: **Imagine that an incredibly wealthy member of our church has just donated a**

LEADER TIP

for The Study

Whenever groups discuss a list of questions, write the questions on newsprint, and tape the newsprint to the wall so groups can discuss the questions at their own pace.

LEADER TIP

for Jackpot!

As students consider how to spend the money, ask them to discuss needs that their charities might be able to fill. For example, if students in your area have too much time with little to do, maybe one charity could provide a fun and interesting after-school activity center.

large portion of her money to you! Each group will be given six million dollars on the condition that it comes up with a plan to spend the money entirely on charity. **In your group, discuss how you want to spend the money. Be creative—you may choose to invent a new charity if you like. The woman has threatened that she will revoke the entire sum if she feels that you are spending the money selfishly.**

The woman also has determined that you must use a portion of the funds to create an advertising campaign for each of your selected charities. So as you decide which charities to give to, create a diagram or a plan for the advertisements you'll include for each charity.

Provide a sheet of newsprint and markers for groups to use to create advertising plans that will convince others to contribute to their charities. After about seven minutes, have groups share their advertisements and plans while describing what they plan to do with the money. Have groups discuss:

● **Which group do you think came up with an interesting idea or an especially good way to spend the money?**

● **Do you ever give to charity? to God? Why or why not?**

● **Do you ever give your talents or time to charity, God, or others? Explain.**

● **Read 2 Corinthians 9:7-8. What are some benefits of giving some of what you have to help others?**

● **Why do we often think we need to have more than enough before we can give any away?**

Ask for a few volunteers who can share a time when they gave money, talents, or time they had to describe their experiences.

Say: **One of the main barriers that prevents us from sharing what God has given us with others is the concern that we won't have enough for ourselves. For example, a person may hesitate to serve at a homeless shelter because the person may be concerned that it will cut into his or her personal time.**

Another barrier to giving our money or talents for God's glory is the feeling that we'll have an opportunity to help at a later time. But <u>Christ could return at any time,</u> so we need to start using the gifts and talents he's given us as soon as possible. We really don't know if we'll have a chance to help at a later time.

BIBLE EXPERIENCE ▼

What Talents? (10 to 15 minutes)
Tape a sheet of newsprint to the wall.

Say: **Another barrier that stops us from giving to others is the belief that we have nothing to give. Sometimes it's hard to believe that God has given us talents or that he would even use us to do his work. Let's shatter this myth by helping each other discover the talents he has given us. What talents has God given us that we can use for his glory?** Have students brainstorm a list of talents while you write each of them on the newsprint. Make sure to leave space

between the talents you list.

When you have about twenty ideas, have kids form groups of four. Say: **Take turns learning about the talents God has given you. Each person should listen as the other three group members tell you which talent from the list is your strongest talent and why they think so. Make sure everyone in your group takes a turn to listen to what the other three group members have to say.**

When groups are done, give each student a "Gifted by God" handout (p. 55) and a pencil. Ask kids to go around the group again, discussing who can benefit from their talents and ways they can use their gifts to minister to others.

Set out colored markers. Say: **When your group has finished, come up to the newsprint and choose one talent that *you* would consider to be a gift you have. Next to the talent, write down one way in which you can use this talent for God's glory. If you and someone else share the same gift, try to come up with different ideas for application.**

When kids finish, say: **It's encouraging to see so many great ways you can use the talents and gifts that God has given you. And you don't have to wait until your talents or gifts are perfected before you can use them. In fact, you should use whatever you have right now to the best of your ability because <u>Christ could return at any time.</u> Other people need to hear about God's love and you need to use your gifts and talents to spread God's message.**

The Parable (15 to 20 minutes)

Have kids return to their trios. Ask students to number off from one to three and go to three designated areas. Assign the following verses to the areas:

● Area One—Matthew 25:14-16, 19-21, 29 (the servant with five talents)
● Area Two—Matthew 25:14-17, 19, 22-23, 29 (the servant with two talents)
● Area Three—Matthew 25:14-15, 18-19, 24-30 (the servant with one talent)

Say: **You're going to look at a story about three people who were given talents (an ancient term for money) from their master. Each group will learn about a different person in the story. Try to become as familiar as you can with your assigned character since**

To grow in our talents, it helps to have someone else who shares the same or similar talent guide us, just as Timothy had Paul to encourage him. Challenge junior highers to find someone with whom they can share their talents and who will encourage them as they grow.

you will be asked to react to a few situations in the same way your character probably would.

Have each group read its assigned passage and discuss:

● **What kind of person is your character?**
● **What kind of attitude do you think he has?**
● **How are you like or unlike your character?**
● **What was the result of your character's actions?**

When students have answered the questions, say: **In a minute, you're going to rejoin your original group. When you do, introduce yourself in character and take turns telling your story, including why you acted the way you did.**

Tell students to get back into their trios. After they introduce their characters, say: **I'm going to read a situation to which you should react in character. Talk with your group about what you think should be done and what you want to do about it. Make sure you answer and act according to the way you think your assigned character would react.** Read the following situations, allowing a minute or so between situations for kids to discuss their reactions:

● **The church is in need of helpers with children's Sunday school.**
● **The homeless shelter needs people to serve meals and distribute clothes.**
● **Your friend needs ten dollars more to go to church camp.**
Then ask:

● **How did you react to the needs of others? Why?**
● **How can we use what we have to produce "more" for God?**
● **What are some ways that we "bury" our abilities?**
Ask students to silently reflect on the following questions:

● **If Jesus were to return tonight, how would you describe the way you've used the talents he gave you?**
● **What do you think he would say to you?**

After a moment, say: **Just as the master in the parable returned home unexpectedly, <u>Christ could return at any time.</u> We need to use the talents he's given us so that one day, we each will hear him say, "Well done, good and faithful servant!"**

"Well Done..." (5 to 10 minutes) Ask a student talented in drama or dramatic reading to read aloud the following story taken from *The Youth Bible* (Word Publishing):

Every Day Counts

Tim Richard was a friend of mine, in an unusual way. We met by accident and had very little in common. We like different foods, different sports, different girls, and we each had our own definition of a "good time." We did share two things, though: we had the same birthday and we loved the same God. Sometimes this was all we could agree on, but we usually enjoyed our time together.

When we were eighteen, Tim died suddenly of a heart attack. He said he wasn't feeling well, and he passed out by the time the paramedics got to him. He was dead hours later. Through my tears, I realized that I didn't have anyone to share my birthday with. And I wasn't so sure about the God that I loved. Why did this happen? Everybody knows that teenagers aren't supposed to die, right?

A few days later, Tim's family and friends got together to mourn his death. As we sat around talking, somebody told a story about Tim that brought a smile to our faces. Before long, all of Tim's old jokes were flying, along with stories of how his short life had touched each of us. In that conversation, we saw that Tim had tried to live each day as though it were an important chance to serve God and others.

I think of my friend Tim often, because his life and death challenged me. I realized I don't know what will happen. So I must work to make each day count.

DEPTHFINDER UNDERSTANDING THE BIBLE

Questions about the second coming of Christ have been discussed since before his death. Mark 13 records a conversation between Jesus and his disciples about the end times. In fact, Mark 13:34-37 contains a parable bearing striking resemblance to the parable of the talents.

However, in this story, the emphasis is noticeably on the servant's vigilant watch for the master's return. Commentator William L. Lane states: "...vigilance rather than calculation is required of the disciples and of the Church....The true servant will want to be actively engaged in his Master's service when he returns."

Our call as Jesus' present-day disciples is to anticipate his return by being obedient servants, using the gifts he's given us to fulfill the work he sets before us prior to his second coming.

Ask:
- **What's your reaction to this story?**
- **Do you know anyone like Tim, who lives every day to serve God and others? How do you feel about that person?**
- **What would it take to challenge you to live your life like Tim lived his?**

Say: **Tim died at a much earlier age than most of us expect to, but none of us know how long we have on this earth, since Christ could return at any time.**

Give each student an "Investing Talents" handout (p. 56) and a pencil.

Say: **Read 1 Corinthians 15:58 then commit to God to use your gifts by completing the sentence, "God has given me the talent of…and I will use it for him by…" Fill in the blanks on your handout, and take the handout home as a reminder.** As a closing prayer, have students stand in a circle and read their commitments by modifying the sentence to read, "God, you have given me the talent of…and I will use it for you by…"

"His master replied, 'Well done, good and faithful servant! You have been faithful with a few things; I will put you in charge of many things. Come and share your master's happiness!'"

—Matthew 25:21

GIFTED by GOD

Possible gifts God has given me:	Possible uses of this gift:
1.	1.
	2.
	3.
2.	1.
	2.
	3.

Investing Talents

"Therefore, my dear brothers, stand firm. Let nothing move you. Always give yourselves fully to the work of the Lord, because you know that your labor in the Lord is not in vain."

—1 Corinthians 15:58

God has given me the talent of _____,

and I will use it for him by _____.

why ▼ Active and Interactive Learning works with teenagers

Let's Start With the Big Picture

Think back to a major life lesson you've learned.
Got it? Now answer these questions:
● Did you learn your lesson from something you read?
● Did you learn it from something you heard?
● Did you learn it from something you experienced?

If you're like 99 percent of your peers, you answered "yes" only to the third question—you learned your life lesson from something you experienced.

This simple test illustrates the most convincing reason for using active and interactive learning with young people: People learn best through experience. Or to put it even more simply, people learn by doing.

Learning by doing is what active learning is all about. No more sitting quietly in chairs and listening to a speaker expound theories about God—that's passive learning. Active learning gets kids out of their chairs and into the experience of life. With active learning, kids get to *do* what they're studying. They *feel* the effects of the principles you teach. They *learn* by experiencing truth firsthand.

Active learning works because it recognizes three basic learning needs and uses them in concert to enable young people to make discoveries on their own and to find practical life applications for the truths they believe.

So what are these three basic learning needs?
1. Teenagers need action.
2. Teenagers need to think.
3. Teenagers need to talk.

Read on to find out exactly how these needs will be met by using the active and interactive learning techniques in Group's Core Belief Bible Study Series in your youth group.

1. Teenagers Need Action

Aircraft pilots know well the difference between passive and active learning. Their passive learning comes through listening to flight instructors and reading flight-instruction books. Their active learning comes through actually flying an airplane or flight simulator. Books and lectures may be helpful, but pilots really learn to fly by manipulating a plane's controls themselves.

We can help young people learn in a similar way. Though we may engage students passively in some reading and listening to teachers, their understanding and application of God's Word will really take off through simulated and real-life experiences.

Forms of active learning include simulation games; role-plays; service projects; experiments; research projects; group pantomimes; mock trials; construction projects; purposeful games; field trips; and, of course, the most powerful form of active learning—real-life experiences.

We can more fully explain active learning by exploring four of its characteristics:

● **Active learning is an adventure.** Passive learning is almost always predictable. Students sit passively while the teacher or speaker follows a planned outline or script.

In active learning, kids may learn lessons the teacher never envisioned. Because the leader trusts students to help create the learning experience, learners may venture into unforeseen discoveries. And often the teacher learns as much as the students.

● **Active learning is fun and captivating.** What are we communicating when we say, "OK, the fun's over—time to talk about God"? What's the hidden message? That joy is separate from God? And that learning is separate from joy?

What a shame.

Active learning is not joyless. One seventh-grader we interviewed clearly remembered her best Sunday school lesson: "Jesus was the light, and we went into a dark room and shut off the lights. We had a candle, and we learned that Jesus is the light and the dark can't shut off the light." That's active learning. Deena enjoyed the lesson. She had fun. And she learned.

Active learning intrigues people. Whether they find a foot-washing experience captivating or maybe a bit uncomfortable, they learn. And they learn on a level deeper than any work sheet or teacher's lecture could ever reach.

● **Active learning involves everyone.** Here the difference between passive and active learning becomes abundantly clear. It's like the difference between watching a football game on television and actually playing in the game.

The "trust walk" provides a good example of involving everyone in active learning. Half of the group members put on blindfolds; the other half serve as guides. The "blind" people trust the guides to lead them through the building or outdoors. The guides prevent the blind people from falling down stairs or tripping over rocks. Everyone needs to participate to learn the inherent lessons of trust, faith, doubt, fear, confidence, and servanthood. Passive spectators of this experience would learn little, but participants learn a great deal.

● **Active learning is focused through debriefing.** Activity simply for activity's sake doesn't usually result in good learning. Debriefing—evaluating an experience by discussing it in pairs or small groups—helps focus the experience and draw out its meaning. Debriefing helps sort and order the information students gather during the experience. It helps learners relate the recently experienced activity to their lives.

The process of debriefing is best started immediately after an experience. We use a three-step process in debriefing: reflection, interpretation, and application.

Reflection—This first step asks the students, "How did you feel?" Active-learning experiences typically evoke an emotional reaction, so it's appropriate to begin debriefing at that level.

Some people ask, "What do feelings have to do with education?" Feelings have everything to do with education. Think back again to that time in your life when you learned a big lesson. In all likelihood, strong feelings accompanied that lesson. Our emotions tend to cement things into our memories.

When you're debriefing, use open-ended questions to probe feelings. Avoid questions that can be answered with a "yes" or "no." Let your learners know that there are no wrong answers to these "feeling" questions. Everyone's feelings are valid.

Interpretation—The next step in the debriefing process asks, "What does this mean to you? How is this experience like or unlike some other aspect of your life?" Now you're asking people to identify a message or principle from the experience.

You want your learners to discover the message for themselves. So instead of telling students your answers, take the time to ask questions that encourage self-discovery. Use Scripture and discussion in pairs or small groups to explore how the actions and effects of the activity might translate to their lives.

Alert! Some of your people may interpret wonderful messages that you never intended. That's not failure! That's the Holy Spirit at work. God allows us to catch different glimpses of his kingdom even when we all look through the same glass.

Application—The final debriefing step asks, "What will you do about it?" This step moves learning into action. Your young people have shared a common experience. They've discovered a principle. Now they must create something new with what they've just experienced and interpreted. They must integrate the message into their lives.

The application stage of debriefing calls for a decision. Ask your students how they'll change, how they'll grow, what they'll do as a result of your time together.

2. Teenagers Need to Think

Today's students have been trained not to think. They aren't dumber than previous generations. We've simply conditioned them not to use their heads.

You see, we've trained our kids to respond with the simplistic answers they think the teacher wants to hear. Fill-in-the-blank student workbooks and teachers who ask dead-end questions such as "What's the capital of Delaware?" have produced kids and adults who have learned not to think.

And it doesn't just happen in junior high or high school. Our children are schooled very early not to think. Teachers attempt to help kids read with nonsensical fill-in-the-blank drills, word scrambles, and missing-letter puzzles.

Helping teenagers think requires a paradigm shift in how we teach. We need to plan for and set aside time for higher-order thinking and be willing to reduce our time spent on lower-order parroting. Group's Core Belief Bible Study Series is designed to help you do just that.

Thinking classrooms look quite different from traditional classrooms. In most church environments, the teacher does most of the talking and hopes that knowledge will transmit from his or her brain to the students'. In thinking settings, the teacher coaches students to ponder, wonder, imagine, and problem-solve.

3. Teenagers Need to Talk

Everyone knows that the person who learns the most in any class is the teacher. Explaining a concept to someone else is usually more helpful to the explainer than to the listener. So why not let the students do more teaching? That's one of the chief benefits of letting kids do the talking. This process is called interactive learning.

What is interactive learning? Interactive learning occurs when students discuss and work cooperatively in pairs or small groups.

Interactive learning encourages learners to work together. It honors the fact that students can learn from one another, not just from the teacher. Students work together in pairs or small groups to accomplish shared goals. They build together, discuss together, and present together. They teach each other and learn from one another. Success as a group is celebrated. Positive interdependence promotes individual and group learning.

Interactive learning not only helps people learn but also helps learners feel better about themselves and get along better with others. It accomplishes these things more effectively than the independent or competitive methods.

Here's a selection of interactive learning techniques that are used in Group's Core Belief Bible Study Series. With any of these models, leaders may assign students to specific partners or small groups. This will maximize cooperation and learning by preventing all the "rowdies" from linking up. And it will allow for new friendships to form outside of established cliques.

Following any period of partner or small-group work, the leader may reconvene the entire class for large-group processing. During this time the teacher may ask for reports or discoveries from individuals or teams. This technique builds in accountability for the teacherless pairs and small groups.

Pair-Share—With this technique each student turns to a partner and responds to a question or problem from the teacher or leader. Every learner responds. There are no passive observers. The teacher may then ask people to share their partners' responses.

Study Partners—Most curricula and most teachers call for Scripture passages to be read to the whole class by one person. One reads; the others doze.

Why not relinquish some teacher control and let partners read and react with each other? They'll all be involved—and will learn more.

Learning Groups—Students work together in small groups to create a model, design artwork, or study a passage or story; then they discuss what they learned through the experience. Each person in the learning group may be assigned a specific role. Here are some examples:

Reader

Recorder (makes notes of key thoughts expressed during the reading or discussion)

Checker (makes sure everyone understands and agrees with answers arrived at by the group)

Encourager (urges silent members to share their thoughts)

When everyone has a specific responsibility, knows what it is, and contributes to a small group, much is accomplished and much is learned.

Summary Partners—One student reads a paragraph, then the partner summarizes the paragraph or interprets its meaning. Partners alternate roles with each paragraph.

The paraphrasing technique also works well in discussions. Anyone who wishes to share a thought must first paraphrase what the previous person said. This sharpens listening skills and demonstrates the power of feedback communication.

Jigsaw—Each person in a small group examines a different concept, Scripture, or part of an issue. Then each teaches the others in the group. Thus, all members teach, and all must learn the others' discoveries. This technique is called a jigsaw because individuals are responsible to their group for different pieces of the puzzle.

JIGSAW EXAMPLE

Here's an example of a jigsaw.

Assign four-person teams. Have teammates each number off from one to four. Have all the Ones go to one corner of the room, all the Twos to another corner, and so on.

Tell team members they're responsible for learning information in their numbered corners and then for teaching their team members when they return to their original teams.

Give the following assignments to various groups:

Ones: Read Psalm 22. Discuss and list the prophecies made about Jesus.

Twos: Read Isaiah 52:13–53:12. Discuss and list the prophecies made

about Jesus.

Threes: Read Matthew 27:1-32. Discuss and list the things that happened to Jesus.

Fours: Read Matthew 27:33-66. Discuss and list the things that happened to Jesus.

After the corner groups meet and discuss, instruct all learners to return to their original teams and report what they've learned. Then have each team determine which prophecies about Jesus were fulfilled in the passages from Matthew.

Call on various individuals in each team to report one or two prophecies that were fulfilled.

You Can Do It Too!

All this information may sound revolutionary to you, but it's really not. God has been using active and interactive learning to teach his people for generations. Just look at Abraham and Isaac, Jacob and Esau, Moses and the Israelites, Ruth and Boaz. And then there's Jesus, who used active learning all the time!

Group's Core Belief Bible Study Series makes it easy for you to use active and interactive learning with your group. The active and interactive elements are automatically built in! Just follow the outlines, and watch as your kids grow through experience and positive interaction with others.

FOR DEEPER STUDY

For more information on incorporating active and interactive learning into your work with teenagers, check out these resources:

● *Why Nobody Learns Much of Anything at Church: And How to Fix It,* by Thom and Joani Schultz (Group Publishing) and
● *Do It! Active Learning in Youth Ministry,* by Thom and Joani Schultz (Group Publishing).

your evaluation of

Bible Study Series
for junior high/middle school

**the truth about
THE LAST DAYS**

Group Publishing, Inc.
Attention: Core Belief Talk-Back
P.O. Box 481
Loveland, CO 80539
Fax: (970) 669-1994

Please help us continue to provide innovative and useful resources for ministry. After you've led the studies in this volume, take a moment to fill out this evaluation; then mail or fax it to us at the address above. Thanks!

● ● ● ● ● ●

1. As a whole, this book has been (circle one)

not very helpful   very helpful
1   2   3   4   5   6   7   8   9   10

2. The best things about this book:

3. How this book could be improved:

4. What I will change because of this book:

5. Would you be interested in field-testing future Core Belief Bible Studies and giving us your feedback? If so, please complete the information below:

Name _____

Street address _____

City _____ State _____Zip _____

Daytime telephone (____) _____ Date _____

THANKS!